The Gospel

According to the Prologue of John

Religion Research Institute Publication

Daniel Amari

Table of Contents

Introduction

In my previous book, *Presenting the Gospel to Muslims*, I encouraged readers to familiarize themselves with a book about the Gospel before engaging with its content. Now, I find it fitting to write a book dedicated to the Gospel itself. With so many excellent works already available on this subject, one might wonder: why another book?

Over the years, I have focused much of my writing and publishing efforts on books about Islam. One of my primary goals has been to equip Christians with resources to effectively present the Gospel to Muslims. However, through this journey, I have realized that it is not enough to provide believers with knowledge about Islam. It is also imperative to equip them with a deep and solid understanding of the Gospel itself. My prayer is that this book will serve as a vital resource for Christians, strengthening their grasp of the Gospel and enabling them to present it effectively, not just with Muslims but with all people.

One important aspect of engaging with Muslims is the need for a Gospel presentation that clearly emphasizes and articulates pivotal doctrines such as the deity of Christ, the Trinity, and the incarnation. Having already authored *John's Logos*, a detailed and advanced study of the Prologue[1] of John written for a more academic audience, it seemed fitting to write a book on the Gospel that makes the profound truths of the Prologue more accessible. While much of the material in this book builds on that earlier work, it has been adapted to better serve a wider readership.

The Prologue of John holds a remarkable quality: it engages with and responds to a variety of opposing worldviews, as though it were written to address the questions of every generation. The timeless truths contained in John 1:1-18 provide a compelling framework to present the Gospel, capable of resonating with people across diverse cultural and philosophical perspectives.

I am deeply indebted to the remarkable advancements in scholarship on John's Gospel, which have provided invaluable insights through technical commentaries. Their work has significantly enriched my understanding and presentation of this text.

These truths, drawn from John's Prologue, remain indispensable today. In the time we are living, the Gospel must be more than a message we share—it must be the foundation of our lives, the bedrock of our families, and the center of our engagement with the world. It is my prayer that this book will inspire you to

---

[1] An introductory section of a text, here referring to the opening verses of the Gospel of John (John 1:1-18), setting the stage for its themes and message.

wholeheartedly embrace the Gospel and equip you to present its truths effectively to everyone you encounter.

The Word

In the beginning was the Word, and the Word was with God, and the Word was God. (John 1:1)

Earlier scholars who published their works in the 20th century debated and discussed the idea that Greek philosophies as represented by Philo,[2] Second Temple wisdom literature, and other Gnostic literature[3] could be possible backgrounds for the Prologue. However, scholars writing in the latter part of the 20th century largely refuted these ideas. Now, 21st-century scholars have moved away from such suggestions, establishing that the Old Testament is the true background of the Prologue.[4] Furthermore, it has been

---

[2] A Jewish philosopher blending Greek thought with Scripture, whose concept of the Logos reflects Platonic influence; see my detailed analysis in *John's Logos*.

[3] Texts emerging from the 2nd century A.D. or later, produced by sects rooted in Platonism infused with Persian ideas and marked by dualism. These writings reinterpret Greek philosophy using Christian and Jewish terms, showing dependence on the Bible and the four Gospels rather than predating them; see my discussion in *Dawn of Islam* (p. 69).

[4] For a detailed exploration of why the Old Testament is the true background of the Prologue, see my earlier work, *John's Logos*.

established that the Gospel of John was written to the Jewish people to tell them that the Messiah of the Old Testament is Jesus.[5]

The word "Logos"[6] has been used extensively in the Septuagint,[7] which is significant because the Septuagint was the Bible of the early church and the Jewish people throughout the region. Greek was the language of the Jewish people in Israel in the 1st century A.D.[8]

Any Jewish person living in the 1st century A.D. who heard the term "Logos" would have immediately thought of the Septuagint, particularly books like Isaiah, where God used His Logos for creation, revelation, and redemption. A study of the Old Testament reveals that within the one Godhead, there is a distinct person often called the Lord (Yahweh, YHWH) who communicated with the people. Given the focus of the Gospel of John on Jesus' acts in new creation, revelation, and redemption, it is understandable that the term "Logos" was used in the Prologue of John.

---

[5] D.A. Carson affirms that John's Gospel aims to show Jews that the Messiah is Jesus, fulfilling Old Testament expectations (e.g., John 20:31). See Carson, *The Gospel According to John*, Pillar New Testament Commentary (Grand Rapids: Eerdmans, 1991), 643-645.

[6] The Greek word translated as 'word' in John 1:1.

[7] The Greek translation of the Old Testament, widely used by Jews and early Christians in the first century A.D.

[8] Stanley E. Porter contends that 'Greek was the language of communication throughout the Eastern Mediterranean world,' with evidence like Greek inscriptions (68% of Jewish epitaphs) showing its pervasive use among Jews in Israel. See Porter, *The Language of the New Testament: Context, History, and Development* (Leiden: Brill, 2013), 67-68.

"In the beginning was the Word." This statement addresses the origin of the Logos. Was He created or formed? Did He emanate from another deity or was He generated by another deity at any time? This verse provides the answer. First, we need to examine the expression "In the beginning." Many suggest it recalls Genesis 1:1 for readers familiar with Scripture, a tie not limited to that verse alone. Proverbs 8, for instance, parallels Genesis 1:1. It is possible that both are intended. The key point is that John's use of "beginning" denotes absolute eternity.[9] Linking Genesis 1:1 with John 1:1 necessitates understanding that eternity in the scriptures refers to the time before the foundation of the earth, before creation, when only God existed, for He alone is uncreated. John 1:1 asserts that the Word was not created, did not become, was not generated, nor emanated; the Word simply was. Remarkably, the Greek word "was" (ἦν, en) used by John is contrasted with "became" (ἐγένετο, egeneto). For instance, in John 8:58, "before Abraham was (ἐγένετο, egeneto), I am (ἦν, en)." In verse 3, describing creation, John uses ἐγένετο (egeneto). In verses 1-2, describing the Son, John uses ἦν (en). In verse 14, describing the incarnation, he uses ἐγένετο (egeneto).

This pattern is powerful and significant, underscoring that the Word was eternal—a truth with profound implications. As only God

---

[9] Time before all creation, belonging to God alone.

is eternal, one must begin with the concept of the eternity of the Son to fully appreciate the Gospel and the incarnation.

"The Word was with God." Several implications arise from this phrase. The first is the usage of the preposition πϱὸς (pros) with. There are other Greek prepositions typically used to indicate 'with,' but πϱὸς (pros) is used in the New Testament to indicate that a person is with a person. This implies that the Logos is an eternal person of God. This statement confirms the Old Testament teaching that there are multiple persons within the one Godhead. Later in the Prologue, the Logos is identified as the Son, and the other person of God is the Father. Furthermore, the insistence on the eternal existence of two persons within the one Godhead together suggests an eternal loving relationship and communion between them. This is confirmed by the rest of the Prologue. It indicates the enormous gift the Father has given us by sacrificing His eternally beloved Son.

The Shema affirms that there is one God, not multiple gods, which is foundational to both the Old and New Testaments. Deuteronomy 6:4 declares, "Hear, O Israel: The Lord our God, the Lord is one." The Hebrew word *echad* ("one") used in the Shema implies a composite unity, as seen elsewhere in Scripture, such as in Genesis 2:24 where "the two become one." This suggests that God's oneness can accommodate distinct persons within the one divine essence. [10] Centuries later, Paul expands upon the Shema in 1 Corinthians 8:6, maintaining monotheism while incorporating Jesus into the divine identity:

Yet for us there is one God, the Father, from whom are all things and for whom we exist, and one Lord, Jesus Christ, through whom are all things and through whom we exist.

In this passage, Paul emphasizes both the oneness of God and the relational distinction within the Godhead, affirming the unity while introducing the distinct personhood of Jesus within that oneness.

In John 1:1b, the phrase "the Word was with God" highlights the eternal loving relationship between the Father and the Son. The Father is the planner and initiator, while the Son is the receiver of love and glory within the Godhead. In this approach, rather than relying on metaphysical distinctions derived from Greek philosophy, [11] the relationship between the Father and the Son is understood primarily through the lens of divine love, focusing on their eternal, loving interaction. While each person of the Trinity has a distinct role, they remain united in essence. There is no subordination or distinction of origin, but rather a harmonious

---

[10] The core nature or being of something; here, it refers to God's single, unified divine nature shared by distinct persons.

[11] Refers mainly to Platonism, which influenced early church fathers with ideas of generation and emanation, suggesting the Son derives from the Father, a view distinct from the relational focus here.

relationship that reflects perfect unity. The Father, Son, and Spirit all share fully in the divine essence, functioning together in perfect accord, bound by eternal love and mutual glorification. Thus, the persons of the Trinity—Father, Son, and Spirit—are distinct not by origin but by relational and functional roles.

"And the Word was God." In Greek, "God" here is definite, identifying the Word as the one true God—not just a divine quality. John chose θεός (theos) that express only the nature of deity, even fully so, showing, as D. A. Carson argues, the Word's identity is God Himself, not merely divine in nature.[12] Now, "God" lacks the Greek article (like "the"), which might suggest it is not definite. But a second consideration refutes this: in Greek, most definite predicate nouns before the verb lack an article, as Graig Keener shows— context must decide.[13] Here, the Old Testament's one-God focus demands it is definite: there is only one God, not many. The missing article also keeps the Word distinct from the Father in John 1:1b, avoiding a mix-up of persons.[14] With remarkable precision, John

---

[12] Carson argues that θεός (theos) is definite, not just 'divine' (for which Greek has θεῖος, theios). See Carson, The Gospel According to John, 117.

[13] Craig S. Keener notes that most definite predicate nominatives before the verb in Greek lack the article (e.g., 87% in one study), so θεός (theos) being anarthrous here is typical. Some see it as qualitative (divine nature), but this book takes it as definite, tying the Word to God's identity. See Keener, The Gospel of John: A Commentary (Peabody, MA: Hendrickson Publishers, 2003), 373, and my work, John's Logos.

[14] Carson adds that the missing article avoids merging the Word with the Father, preserving distinction. See Carson, The Gospel According to John, 117, and my work, John's Logos.

articulates the deity of Christ, balancing His identity as God with His distinction from the Father.

He was in the beginning with God. (John 1:2)

For verse 2, "He was in the beginning with God," older translations render this as "this," since the Greek οὗτος (houtos) can be a demonstrative pronoun meaning "this," "this one," or "he." Modern translations favor "he," giving the Word a clear personal identity. More importantly, nearly all commentators see verse 2 as a summary of verse 1, restating that the Word was with God from the beginning, while preparing for verse 3's focus on creation. John uses this repetition to ensure the Word's divine status is unmistakable, a point he echoes in verse 18 by placing the Son at the Father's side as the only God.

From John 1:1-2 emerge foundational truths about God. There is one God alone, as the Old Testament affirms, yet this one God exists as multiple persons—the Word with God and as God. Each person, the Father and the Son here revealed, is distinct in relationship yet united in their single divine essence, each fully and eternally God. Between them flows an eternal love, a communion unbroken before creation began. These principles, drawn from the Word's eternity, deity, and distinction, establish the doctrine of the Trinity, the bedrock of the Gospel that John proclaims.

The greatest sacrifice of the eternal Son who is beloved from the Father from eternity invites from us everlasting worship, consecration, and love. The Gospel is not just about what Jesus taught and did on earth. It goes beyond that, starting from eternity, where the eternal Son of God existed before creation.

Theological Implications

In the beginning was the Word, and the Word was with God, and the Word was God. He was in the beginning with God. (John 1:1-2)

Let us not overlook the overarching message of these verses. As established in Chapter 1, the purpose of this passage, and indeed the entire Gospel, is to present to the Jewish people that the Messiah is Jesus. In other words, John's initial step in presenting the gospel to this community was to articulate the doctrine of the Trinity. This approach parallels the first chapter of Ephesians, by highlighting the roles of the Father in election, the Son in redemption, and the Spirit in sealing our salvation. This affirms that the Gospel is fundamentally Trinitarian, starting with and emphasizing the doctrine of the Trinity.

Furthermore, we should not overlook the depth and profound nature of John's Trinitarian presentation of the Gospel. While modern wisdom often echoes the mantra "simplify, simplify," the first verse introduces a profound theology that must not be weakened for the sake of superficial presentation.

Clarity in presenting the deity of Christ and the Trinity is foundational to the Gospel. One cannot effectively present the Gospel without first establishing a clear understanding of

Christology. Many avoid discussing the doctrines of the Trinity and the deity of Christ, thinking that delaying these topics will reduce objections and increase acceptance. However, the Gospel does not function this way. John begins the Gospel message with the doctrines of the Trinity and the deity of Christ. He repeatedly emphasizes these points to ensure the Gospel's full truth is grasped, a priority that reveals their necessity for faith and proclamation. Despite knowing his audience had significant difficulties with these doctrines, John prioritizes them from the outset.

Why deep theology? The Word of God, with its rich theology of the deity of Christ and the Trinity, is the essential seed that brings about true change. While we believe in the power of prayer and acknowledge that God has ordained other factors to nurture the seed, these are merely the means of watering it. Imagine soil that is regularly watered and optimally fertilized but lacks any seed or the correct seed; no growth can be expected regardless of how much care it receives. The presence of the right seed is vital. Thus, the best way to evaluate a ministry is by the quality of the seed planted, not by the visible fruits produced. Focusing solely on visible fruits can lead to the rise of cults and false religions and is not a responsible stewardship of God's resources.

In John's presentation of the doctrine of the Trinity, it is deeply consequential that he did not rely on analogies from creation to illustrate the Triune God. He avoided using elements like human, sun, or egg that could oversimplify the incomprehensible nature of the Trinity. Additionally, John refrained from drawing on Greek philosophical categories to explain or build bridges to the doctrine, despite the influence of such philosophies during the 1st century. Instead, his explanation of the Trinity is rooted entirely in divine revelation, drawing from Scripture, as seen in the first chapter's Old Testament roots, to articulate the eternal relationship between the Father, Son, and Spirit. John's theological depth comes from the revealed truth of God's Word, rather than external systems of thought or natural analogies.

The Triune nature of God uniquely preserves both transcendence—His existence beyond creation—and monotheism. God's transcendence is upheld through the eternal relationship within the Trinity—Father, Son, and Holy Spirit—which demonstrates that God exists in perfect harmony within Himself, independent of the created world. This ensures that God remains beyond human comprehension and above creation. At the same time, the Trinity affirms strict monotheism—one God alone—by declaring that the Father, Son, and Holy Spirit are not three separate gods but one God in three distinct persons. This doctrine prevents any drift into polytheism—the belief in many gods—while maintaining God's unity. Without the Trinity, either transcendence or monotheism would be compromised, but the doctrine holds both together in perfect balance.

The Triune nature of God uniquely preserves both transcendence and monotheism. God's transcendence is upheld through the eternal relationship within the Trinity—Father, Son, and Holy Spirit—which demonstrates that God exists in perfect harmony within Himself, independent of the created world. This ensures that God remains beyond human comprehension and above creation. At the same time, the Trinity affirms strict monotheism by declaring that the Father, Son, and Holy Spirit are not three separate gods but one God in three distinct persons. This doctrine prevents any drift into polytheism while maintaining God's unity. Without the Trinity, either transcendence or monotheism would be compromised, but the doctrine holds both together in perfect balance.

The Triune nature of God preserves both His monotheism and the perfection of His attributes, particularly His eternal love. Within the Trinity, the Father and the Son exist in an eternal loving relationship, ensuring that God has always been loving, even before creation. Without the Trinity, a monotheistic God, existing alone, could not express or experience love until He created other beings to receive it. This would mean God's love began only with creation, implying it was not eternal and that He lacked this attribute from eternity past. Such a limitation would challenge His perfection, suggesting that key attributes like love and unchanging nature were incomplete until creation altered Him. Trinitarian monotheism, however, maintains God's eternal consistency, as the love between the Father, Son, and Spirit within the Godhead ensures that God is both one and eternally complete in love, without dependence on creation.

As an application for the Christian life, sound theology is not necessarily an indication of true spirituality. A person can have good and sound theology without possessing the spiritual life that manifests in holiness, humility, and consecration to the Lord. However, I am highly skeptical of claims of spiritual life characterized by holiness, humility, and consecration without a true foundational theology. My reading of Scripture tells me that God only builds on the biblical theological foundation of His Word. My experience has shown that God works through me spiritually as I gain a deeper understanding of Scripture. Claims of spiritual experience without in-depth scriptural knowledge are suspect. If you desire to grow in the Lord, grow in His Word.

If you desire spiritual growth in your family, invest in a deeper theological understanding of the Word of God. Prioritize Scripture and sound theology. While theology alone does not guarantee spirituality, neglecting it ensures a lack of spiritual growth. Just as sowing and watering seeds do not guarantee a harvest, nevertheless they are essential steps; without them, a harvest is impossible.

Find a way to instill the Word of God in your children. Read the Bible with them every day, exegeting Scripture and sharing deep theology. Establish a nightly routine of reading Scripture together. Additionally, create a family altar [15] where you explore the rich insights and deeper theology of God's Word. For single people, before marriage, seek a commitment from your future spouse to maintain a daily family altar where the Word of God will be taught.

For one's soul, the Word of God is the source of hope in a world often devoid of it. During difficult times when comfort and consolation are needed, the Holy Spirit guides individuals to drink from the richness of God's Word and its theological depths. There, one begins to understand the consistency and unfailing nature of God's character and the certainty of His purpose, which becomes the source of hope. If one seeks growth, consecration, and holiness, it is in the richness of God's word and its profound theology that nourishment and blessing are found.

Do not study theology merely to increase your knowledge or to present yourself as an expert before others. Instead, seek the theology of Scripture to worship the Lord, love Him more, and persevere in hope.

---

[15] The concept of a family altar refers to a set time for families to gather in worship, prayer, and the study of God's Word at home.

The Creator

All things came to be through Him, and without Him nothing came into being that was made. *(John 1:3)*

The Old Testament describes Yahweh as the creator of all things alone by Himself (c.f. Isaiah 44:24 and Genesis 1). At the same time, it describes multiple persons all involved in creation. Within the eternal council of the Trinity, the Father decrees the plan of creation, the Son brings it into being as its craftsman, and the Spirit sustains it with life. The Father plans all that exists, drawing out the heavens and earth as their designer (Proverbs 8:27; Psalm 33:6), the Son, as Wisdom, shapes everything that God designed (Proverbs 8:22-31), and the Spirit hovers over the formless void to infuse it with order and vitality (Genesis 1:2). According to Colossians 1:15-16, Christ is the creator of everything, and all things were created for Him and through Him. Christ is described as the Amen, the faithful witness, in Revelation 3:14, a reference to the Amon, or master craftsman, of Proverbs 8.[16] As such, this verse emphasizes the deity of Christ.

Furthermore, this verse highlights the role of Christ in creation. When it comes to creation, the Son created all that was created. In presenting the Gospel, John emphasizes the relationship of Christ to creation reminding us that the universe is not eternal. It had a beginning which is confirmed by the use of the verb "became" (ἐγένετο, egeneto). Moreover, there is a purpose for creation in the fact that Christ is the true owner of creation, having created the whole world. We do not live in a random world. But we live in God's world, the one who works all things according to the councel of His will.

This truth redirects our focus from a self-centered existence to the purpose unveiled in Christ's creative work. The sublime implication of verse 3 is that the world was created with a higher purpose, grounded in the fact that it was made by Christ and for Christ. Since Christ is the creator of everything, humanity is not the center of the universe; Christ is. Therefore, people should not live for themselves but should align their lives with the purpose of Christ, seeking His glory in all they do.

Furthermore, since Christ created all things, it establishes that the Triune God has decreed everything from eternity. This is

---

[16] For a deeper discussion of Christ as the Amon and Wisdom in creation, see my work, *John's Logos*.

consistent with Ephesians 1:11 when it declares that God works all things according to the counsel of His will. For believers, this is a comforting truth: the Lord works out everything for the good of His children according to His divine purpose (Romans 8:28).

When you look at the world and its affairs, do not be discouraged. God is administering everything at the right time to fulfill His goal of summing up all things under Christ, both in heaven and on earth. Likewise, when you face personal circumstances and difficult trials, trust that God is working all things for good. This reveals the enduring relationship between Christ, the Creator, and His creation—an order established for His glory, now upheld by His sovereign care despite its present struggles.

The Life and the Light

In him was life, and the life was the light of men. The light shines in the darkness, and the darkness has not conquered it. (John 1:4-5)

"In Him was life." Notably, the verb used here is "was," consistent with verses 1 and 2, and unlike the "became" in verse 3. This indicates that life was eternally in the Son. According to the Gospel of John, life signifies eternal life. These qualities are attributes of God, not created but eternally inherent to Him. Thus, Christ is the source of eternal life, and there is no spiritual life without a connection to Him.

This calls to mind Adam and Eve in the garden. God warned them that disobedience would result in immediate spiritual death, meaning the severance of their spiritual relationship with the Lord Jesus Christ.

In the Gospel of John, light represents truth, encompassing spiritual enlightenment and holiness. Significantly, truth cannot be attained apart from the spiritual life that is in Christ—it comes through His life alone, not through human effort apart from Him. Spiritual life is the prerequisite for spiritual truth.

When presenting the Gospel, it needs be recognized that an unregenerate heart does not seek God or the truth. No amount of theoretical attempts will enlighten the mind to the truth of God. Spiritual truth comes only from the life that Christ provides.

Furthermore, it should be communicated as part of presenting the Gospel that understanding the Gospel requires God to give life first, and Christ is the only source of that life.

Ephesians 1:4 states that God the Father chose us in Christ before the foundation of the world to be holy and blameless before Him in love. From verse 3, we learn that Christ created the world, indicating a divine purpose for all things. This purpose is now more deeply understood as having a personal, loving relationship with Christ. As the source of spiritual life, Christ is the source for anyone to experience true life; without a personal relationship with Him, there is no life.

This concept extends beyond presenting the gospel to non-believers; it defines our purpose and calling as believers. We were chosen to stand before the Lord, holy and blameless in love, for eternity. In other words, we are called to a personal relationship with the Lord. Even as believers, we cannot function properly without daily communion with Christ. Though we are born again, we are not the source of life; Christ is the source of life.

The term "darkness" denotes to the spiritual darkness of the world since the fall. The light of Christ, or Christ Himself, has always shone. In the context of this gospel, this Light shone even more strongly and clearly through the incarnation. Despite this, the darkness could not overcome or conquer the Light. The Gospel of John states that people loved darkness more than Light because their deeds were evil. However, this is not a pagan or philosophical dualism—these are not equal forces. The message is clear: darkness failed to overcome the Light, and the Light was victorious. This does not mean that everyone will believe in the Light, but the Light has its own children—those who will believe.

This is part of the gospel message that communicates the state of the fallen world—a sinful world that hates truth and hates Christ. It is not merely ignorant of the truth; it hates the truth because it delights in sin. At the same time, the gospel message conveys hope: the darkness did not overcome the Light. The Light is victorious, and Christ has accomplished His mission.

There came a man sent from God, named John. (John 1:6)

Observe that when discussing John the Baptist, the verb ἐγένετο (became) is used to describe his coming. This highlights John the beloved's intention to maintain focus on the Logos and to clearly distinguish who is God and who is not.

Why mention John the Baptist when discussing the Logos? John the Baptist is vital for the start of Jesus' public ministry. His baptism was so pivotal that it is emphasized in the synoptic gospels, and witnessing it was a requirement for replacing Judas among the apostles. But why was John's baptism and testimony about Christ so crucial? The answer is that God promised in the Old Testament to send a forerunner before He comes to visit His people.

The application here is that the Lord works within the foundation of the Old Testament that He laid. This is evident when Peter preached the Gospel to Cornelius, including the baptism of John, and when Paul preached in the synagogue in Pisidian Antioch, also mentioning John's baptism. This clearly suggests that the presentation of the Gospel requires the Old Testament. In fact, the Old Testament provides the dimension of consistency, demonstrating that God's message and promises are consistent throughout history. The gospel message of Christ did not emerge in isolation; it was supported by prophecy over thousands of years of God's dealings with His people.

If the Old Testament is necessary for presenting the Gospel, then it is equally important for our lives and for our children. Teaching our children the Old Testament establishes the necessary foundation in their hearts for receiving and comprehending the good news of the Gospel—revealing humanity's sin and God's promised rescue, woven through its history and fulfilled in Christ.

The Old Testament serves as God's foundation for imparting divine truths to humanity, truths that require preparation to fully grasp the Gospel's message. It is a vast repository of spiritual principles—drawn from thousands of years of salvation history—designed to build understanding of humanity's need and God's redemptive plan. From Adam's fall revealing sin's cost to the sacrifices foreshadowing Christ's atonement, these accounts and patterns lay the groundwork across generations, ensuring the Gospel stands on a foundation prepared by God Himself.

He came as a witness in order to bear witness to the Light, in order that all believe through him. (John 1:6)

Notice that John the Baptist's mission was to serve as a witness. While Christ did not need a human witness, it was necessary because of the world's darkness. John's primary role was to point to Christ so that all might believe in Him through John's testimony. As Leon Morris observed:

This emphasis on testimony should not be minimized. Testimony is a serious matter and the means of substantiating the truth of a matter; there is a legal air about it. It is clear that our author wants his readers to take what he writes as reliable. He is insistent that there is good evidence for the things he sets down. Witness establishes the truth.[17]

This reliance on testimony reveals the value of apologetics[18] in presenting the Gospel. By offering reasoned answers, apologetics enables us to affirm the truth to non-believers, communicating answers despite a world resistant to John's witness—where many reject it, yet some accept. Furthermore, apologetics equips our children to stand firm in truth. Beyond aiding outreach, it establishes them in faith, ensuring they grasp the Gospel's reliability amid doubt.

He was not the Light, but to witness concerning the Light. (John 1:8)

As much as John the Baptist plays an important role for us in witnessing about the Light, we are reminded that he is not the Light. The Lord uses witnesses to lead us to Him. Yet we need to recall that they are unworthy servants doing the bidding of the Lord. Our loyalty, love, and attachment belong to Christ alone. Likewise, the Lord might use us to lead, help, or shepherd others to Him. Yet we

---

[17] Leon Morris, *The Gospel of John*, New International Commentary on the New Testament. (Grand Rapids: Eerdmans, 1995), 80.

[18] Apologetics refers to the reasoned defense of the Christian faith, equipping believers to answer questions and affirm truth.

should always guard against assuming any role greater than being witnesses of Him. We are not the Light. He is the Light. A striking example was John the Baptist who said of Christ, "He must increase and I must decrease." (John 3:30)

The genuine Light, which gives light to every man, was coming into the world. (John 1:9)

If John the Baptist was not the Light but a witness to the Light, then who is the Light? The Logos is the Light. Notice how the focus is on the Son and His glory. Furthermore, He is the true Light. The term "true" here, and in the context of Scripture, means that the Word is "the genuine and ultimate self-disclosure of God to man."[19] God spoke in many ways, but in the last days, He spoke to us through His Son (Hebrews 1:1-2). The phrase "that lights every man" indicates that Christ is the sole source of truth for all. There are flickering, dim, and tainted reflectors, but none can be described as the genuine Light.

But why focus on the glory of the Son? Because the Son is the radiance of God's glory and the exact imprint of His nature (Hebrews 1:3). The phrase "coming to this world" is used in the Gospel of John to describe the incarnation. Therefore, the incarnation of the Son is the ultimate disclosure of God.

---

[19]Carson, *The Gospel* According to John, 122.

Finding guidance in your life, bringing truth to your family, and leading someone to faith requires recognizing that Christ alone is the ultimate source of Light. Since He is the Light, direct them to Jesus. No amount of information can illuminate a person; only an encounter with Christ can. Invest in opportunities for others to hear about Christ, read His Word, and spend time with Him in prayer.

The Tragedy

¹⁰ He was in the world, and the world came into being through Him, yet the world did not know Him.

The world's failure to know its Creator, who made it to reflect His glory, marks a dire tragedy. The use of a masculine pronoun substantiates the context of the text, emphasizing that the Light is indeed a person. Additionally, there is a parallelism between the creation of all things by the Word in verse 3 and the creation of the world by the Light in verse 10. This reveals Christ as a personal Creator whom the world should honor, yet its refusal to acknowledge Him deepens the tragedy of its rebellion. John does not hesitate to state that Christ created the world. Unlike dualistic systems—beliefs that pit an evil creator against a good one, attributing the world's flaws to a lesser power—John boldly affirms that God created the world.[20] If Greek philosophies or similar systems had influenced

---

[20] Dualistic systems, common in Greek-influenced thought, often separate a higher good from a flawed material world, sometimes attributing creation to a lesser power. John's Gospel stands apart, affirming Christ as the sole Creator of all.

John, we would have seen him avoid the language that attributes creation of the world directly to God. John unequivocally holds the world accountable for its evil deeds. As the Creator present in the world, Christ deserves its honor, yet it failed to give it—a stark tragedy.[21] The world loved darkness more than the Light because their deeds were evil (John 3:19).

Part of presenting the Gospel is being candid about the tragedy of the world: it is rebellious and hateful of God. Despite God becoming human and visiting this world, the world failed to honor its Creator. The good news of the Gospel includes the grim truth about the darkness and evil of the world.

There is a pressing application to our lives here. It is a deep tragedy when Christ and a relationship with Him are neglected within

---

[21] Scholars debate Christ's presence in this verse. Carson writes, 'The most natural way to take v. 10 is as a reference to the incarnation... The Word was in the world—not just paying a visit, but residing here' (*The Gospel According to John*, 124). Yet ἦν ('was') over ἐγένετο ('became') prompts questions. Morris notes, 'The verb "was" (ἦν) suggests more than a fleeting visit; it implies a continuing presence' (*The Gospel of John*, 84). Colin G. Kruse adds, 'Looking back from a post-resurrection perspective, the evangelist writes, "He was in the world," reflecting on the time when the Word entered it' (*John: An Introduction and Commentary*, vol. 4 of Tyndale New Testament Commentaries, IVP [Downers Grove: InterVarsity Press, 2003], 67). Gerald L. Borchert asserts, 'This verse presupposes the incarnation... The use of ἦν rather than ἐγένετο stresses that the Word was not part of the created order but distinct from it' (*John 1–11*, eds. E. Ray Clendenen and David S. Dockery, vol. 25A of The New American Commentary [Nashville: Broadman & Holman Publishers, 1996], 113). Likely, ἦν and ἐγένετο flex with context—here signaling the Word's incarnation among us.

our families. The situation becomes even more lamentable when our children grow up with little regard for their spiritual life in Christ.

11 He came to his own, and his own did not receive him.

Not only did the world fail to recognize its Creator, but even the people of God, who were supposed to belong to Him, did not receive Him. The long history of God's Old Testament dealings with the people of Israel should have made them even more receptive to welcoming and accepting the Son of God. No one can overlook the rich history of God's graciousness and faithfulness towards Israel. If any group of people should have welcomed Him, it should have been them. However, that was not the case, and the rest of the world fares no differently. The Jewish nation represents humanity as a whole. The point is that no matter how many times God has blessed, revealed Himself to, and helped humanity, they have not received Him.

The Good News

¹² But to all who received Him, He gave right to become children of God, to those who believe in His name.

In contrast to the world's rejection of the Son of God, there stands a remnant characterized by their reception of Him and belief in His name. In the Old Testament, "name" serves as a circumlocution for God, implying belief in His deity. Moreover, His name signifies the totality of attributes. Thus, believing in His name encompasses trust and dependence on every aspect of the Son of God: His grace, love, justice, works, and all His attributes.

The term "gave" implies grace, a fully unmerited gift from God. It signifies that the remnant's belief and what they received from God are entirely due to His grace. He granted them authority—not the choice to accept or reject, but rather the status and right to become privileged members of the people of the covenant, adopted children of God. In Greek, the term for children of God differs from that used for Christ as the Son of God, a distinction maintained throughout the Gospel of John to highlight Christ's unique status within its context.

Notice that the most widely recognized and presented part of the gospel message—receiving Christ—is actually presented later in the prologue of John, not first. There is often a misconception that beginning with this call to belief demonstrates faithfulness to the Lord. However, consider that there are 11 verses preceding verse 12 in John's Gospel. Before urging people to believe in Christ, it is exigent to first establish His identity. Furthermore, the Gospel message unfolds with additional truths and explanations. Given that the Gospel of John was written for Jewish readers familiar with the Old Testament, these initial verses are foundational. They address significant challenges and misunderstandings that 1st-century Jews had regarding Christ. Starting with these foundational truths makes it the most direct presentation of the Gospel, addressing its most challenging aspects from the outset.

> *13 They were born, not of blood nor of the will of the flesh nor of the will of man, but of God.*

When discussing what sets apart the minority who believed when the world did not, the explanation lies in their being born again. Here is the breakdown: First, it is not by human will—specifically, not by lineage, as seen in the reference to descent from Abraham. This implies that being born into a godly lineage does not guarantee faith in subsequent generations. Second, it is not by human decision or effort; it does not originate from any humanly devised system. Third, it is by the will of God alone. It is His choice, His initiative, and His sovereign prerogative. Fourth, when all these aspects come together, it constitutes a spiritual birth. This is not a physical action but a spiritual work of God in the heart, resulting in faith and repentance. This sheds light on why some believe while others do not.

The Glory of Yahweh

The LORD said to Moses, "Depart; go up from here, you and the people whom you have brought up out of the land of Egypt, to the land of which I swore to Abraham, Isaac, and Jacob, saying, 'To your offspring I will give it.' 2 I will send an angel before you, and I will drive out the Canaanites, the Amorites, the Hittites, the Perizzites, the Hivites, and the Jebusites. 3 Go up to a land flowing with milk and honey; but I will not go up among you, lest I consume you on the way, for you are a stiff-necked people."
(Exodus 33:1-3)

To better grasp John 1:14, we must examine the accounts in Exodus 33-34. Chapter 33 begins in the aftermath of the golden calf incident. Moses, in dialogue with the Lord, sought to salvage the situation after the people of Israel had gravely sinned against God. This exchange was directed by the Lord toward a prophetic purpose, ultimately fulfilled in the incarnation of the Son in John's Gospel, and articulated in the Prologue of John. In an interaction resembling a negotiation, the Lord pledged to honor His covenant with the patriarchs by granting the Israelites the land flowing with milk and honey and expelling all their adversaries. However, there was a grave condition: the Lord would not be with them. Their sin was so severe that His presence would lead to their complete destruction. Instead, He would send an angel to go before them.

It holds profound importance that the text refers to "an angel" in this context. When the Lord Himself went before the people of Israel, the one sent was called "The Angel of the Lord," and He was described as having the name of Yahweh within Him. This indicates that the one sent bore within Himself the entirety of God's attributes. Stated differently, within the oneness of the singular God, the one sent possesses full deity, yet remains distinct from the Sender, who likewise embodies full deity. In Isaiah, this person is referred to as the "Angel of His Presence." This is why the Israelites understood that the Angel of the Lord was Yahweh Himself.

When the people heard this disastrous word, they mourned, and no one put on his ornaments. (*Exodus 33:4*)

From a purely earthly perspective, the Lord's proposal to the Israelites appeared exceedingly advantageous. He would drive out their enemies and deliver the land He had promised to the patriarchs. An angel would go before them to ensure all of this came to pass. Yet, to the people of Israel, this was a devastating message. They understood that the Lord's presence was their most valuable possession. The prospect of losing His presence was unbearable, leading them to mourn deeply.

Moses said to the LORD, "See, you say to me, 'Bring up this people,' but you have not let me know whom you will send with me. Yet you have said, 'I know you by name, and you have also found favor in my sight.' 13 Now therefore, if I have found favor in your sight, please show me now your ways, that I may know you in order to find favor in your sight. Consider too that this nation is your people." 14 And he said, "My presence will go with you, and I will give you rest."
(Exodus 33:12-14)

Moses appealed to the Lord on behalf of himself and the people of Israel, seeking the Lord's own presence to go with them instead of merely an angel. Moses grounded his appeal in the favor and grace of the Lord. In response, the Lord reassured Moses that His presence would indeed go with them, granting them rest and guiding them forward personally.

And he said to him, "If your presence will not go with me, do not bring us up from here. For how shall it be known that I have found favor in your sight, I and your people? Is it not in your going with us, so that we are distinct, I and your people, from every other people on the face of the earth?" And the LORD said to Moses, "This very thing that you have spoken I will do, for you have found favor in my sight, and I know you by name." Moses said, "Please show me your glory."
(Exodus 33:15-18)

Even after the Lord consented to go before them, Moses repeated his appeal. The Lord, in His grace, reaffirmed His commitment. But why did Moses feel the need to reiterate his request? It appears that Moses, deeply troubled by the gravity of Israel's transgression and keenly aware of God's holiness and justice, sought greater assurance. He understood that the people's transgression was severe, so he sought a tangible demonstration of God's glory. Moses yearned to behold the fullness of God's attributes, particularly His covenantal love, grace, and faithfulness, as an assurance that the Lord would truly forgive and be merciful toward them.

And he said, "I will make all my goodness pass before you and will proclaim before you my name 'The LORD.' And I will be gracious to whom I will be gracious, and will show mercy on whom I will show mercy.
(Exodus 33:19)

In this verse, the Lord emphasizes that His grace and mercy are not rooted in human worthiness but in His own sovereign will. He says, "I will make all my goodness pass before you and will proclaim before you my name The Lord." This statement highlights two key aspects: God's goodness and His name. God's goodness refers to the totality of His character—His love, justice, mercy, and faithfulness. His name, Yahweh, encapsulates His eternal, unchanging nature and His covenantal faithfulness to His people. The foundation of grace lies in the very nature of God, not in the merit of humans. Yet Moses is also reminded of God's holiness and transcendence, as the Lord declares that Moses cannot see His full glory and live. Even so, God mercifully provides a way for Moses to experience a glimpse of His glory, protecting him from the overwhelming power of His presence.

The LORD descended in the cloud and stood with him there, and proclaimed the name of the LORD. 6 The LORD passed before him and proclaimed, "The LORD, the LORD, a God merciful and gracious, slow to anger, and abounding in steadfast love and faithfulness, (Exodus 34:5-6)

It bears immense weight that the Lord chose to descend to proclaim His own name. While God could have revealed His name to Moses without descending, He deliberately chose to do so. This act assuredly carries prophetic significance. In His proclamation, the Lord emphasized a key description that resonates throughout the Old Testament: "abounding in steadfast love and faithfulness." This became a defining characteristic of Yahweh, shaping how He was understood and worshipped. The language of God's steadfast love and faithfulness reverberates through books like the Psalms, Isaiah, Jeremiah, and others, serving as a central theme in Israel's theology and worship. The Psalms, in particular, repeatedly praise Yahweh for His steadfast love and faithfulness, and this description becomes a bedrock of covenantal understanding across prophetic and poetic texts alike.

keeping steadfast love for thousands, forgiving iniquity and
transgression and sin, but who will by no means clear the guilty,
visiting the iniquity of the fathers on the children and the children's
children, to the third and the fourth generation."
(Exodus 34:7)

The Lord assures that He will forgive, but He will not leave the guilty unpunished. This reveals that the forgiveness God extends is not without cost, requiring the satisfaction of His holiness and justice. While the text does not explain how this will be accomplished, it points forward to the cross, where both grace and justice, mercy and holiness, converge in the ultimate fulfillment of God's plan.

And Moses quickly bowed his head toward the earth and worshiped.
(Exodus 34:8)

In the presence of the highest manifestation of God's glory ever revealed in the Old Testament, Moses' immediate and only fitting response was to bow in worship.

And he said, "If now I have found favor in your sight, O Lord,
please let the Lord go in the midst of us, for it is a stiff-necked people,
and pardon our iniquity and our sin, and take us for your
inheritance."
(Exodus 34:9)

One remarkable observation in this verse is Moses addressing Yahweh, asking Him to send Yahweh to dwell in the midst of the people of Israel. In essence, it is Yahweh sending Yahweh. Previously, we saw Yahweh sending the Angel of the Lord, who bears His name and attributes. This profound passage points to the Triune nature of the one God, foreshadowing a deeper revelation of God's unity and distinction within the Godhead.

Glory of the Son

And the Word became flesh and dwelt among us, and we have seen his glory, glory as of the unique beloved Son from the Father, full of grace and truth. (John 1:14)

"And the Word became flesh." Observe initially the intentional use of the verb "became" (ἐγένετο, egeneto). It signifies a definitive moment in history when the Word took on flesh. Across John's Prologue, a consistent selection of verbs highlights this distinction. Next, the Greek term sarx (σὰρξ, flesh) decisively rejects any alignment with dualistic Hellenistic frameworks or comparable philosophies. Furthermore, although the term "flesh" sharply diverges from Hellenistic notions, it expresses a momentous truth: the eternal God, who fashioned the cosmos, has remarkably taken on complete humanity, sin excepted. This revelation would have been profoundly startling to readers in the 1st century.

"And dwelt among us." The Greek term eskenosen (ἐσκήνωσεν, dwelt) evokes two key elements from the Old Testament. First, it recalls the tabernacle (mishkān), the sacred place where God dwelt with His covenant people, and where His glory filled the tabernacle.

Second, it echoes Yahweh's promises to dwell with His people. This resplendent event realizes the types and prophecies of the Old Testament, fulfilling entirely the aspirations of God's people and every promise declared. In Christ, these ancient hopes find their ultimate fulfillment.

When presenting the Gospel, one should emphasize how Christ fulfills the prophecies and types found in the Old Testament, revealing Him as the long-awaited Messiah and the embodiment of the promises made to God's people throughout history.

"And we have seen his glory." Note that it specifies that "we" - not the world - have seen his glory. This primarily refers to the disciples who witnessed firsthand the signs Christ performed during His earthly ministry, especially highlighting the significance of the cross and resurrection. In these events, the glory of God the Son, and thereby God Himself, shone most brightly. Additionally, believers in the Son also experience His glory. Why do solely believers perceive the glory of God, while the entire world remains excluded? The answer lies in God's work in their lives.

Glory as of the unique beloved Son from the Father: The phrase "unique beloved" here is monogenous (μονογενοῦς from μονογενής, monogenēs). When examining this term in relation to the Old Testament, it translates the Hebrew term yāḥîd. A notable example is Isaac, described as the "only Son" using this term. In the book of Hebrews, yāḥîd is rendered as monogenēs, conveying the meaning of "unique and beloved." Moreover, monogenēs appears in two significant instances in the New Testament Gospels: Jairus's daughter and the Widow of Nain, where it signifies "only" with a beloved connotation. Significantly, no Hellenistic writings, Christian or otherwise, employ monogenēs to signify "begotten." Moreover, early Church Fathers, notwithstanding their diverse views on the Son's generation—eternal or otherwise—refrained from using this term to indicate generation, opting instead for distinct terminology. Thus, rendering monogenēs as "only-begotten" under any circumstance proves wholly erroneous.[22]

But what glory is this? It is the glory of the Son, who is uniquely beloved by the Father. This glory manifests the attributes of the Triune God, stemming from the eternal loving relationship within the Trinity. So, what does the cross communicate to us? It reveals the immense depth of divine love shared between the Father and the Son. Through the Father's gift of His Son to us, we behold the boundless measure of His love—granting us His unique beloved Son.

"Full of grace and truth." This phrase recalls Exodus 33 and 34, where Moses implored Yahweh to reveal His glory. In response, God shielded Moses from His full glory, protecting him from death. The

---

[22] Cf. *John's Logos*, which provides a comprehensive treatment of the usage of monogenes across all Hellenistic literature.

Lord positioned Moses within a cleft of the rock, permitting him to perceive a glimpse as God passed by, proclaiming Himself abundant in steadfast love and faithfulness.

In Exodus, we see the declaration of multiple persons within the one God, demonstrating how God the Son, one person of Triune God, reveals the glory of the one God to humanity. Steadfast love signifies God's unmerited covenantal favor, while faithfulness underscores His reliability and fidelity to Himself. John translates these terms into grace and truth.

So, what constitutes the glory of God? It is His goodness as revealed in His attributes—grace and faithfulness. Where have we seen these attributes most vividly displayed? It is in the cross. The presence of the incarnate Son signifies Yahweh dwelling among His people, attributing to the Son qualities that are uniquely divine and embodying "those stabilizing divine qualities God's people have repeatedly experienced."[23]

15 John bore witness about Him and cried out, 'This is He of whom I said, "He who comes after me is superior to me because He was before me."

---

[23] Borchert, *John 1–11*, 121.

In light of Yahweh's extraordinary glory and the great significance of His incarnation, John the Baptist's testimony reveals this truth. John declares Jesus' superiority, stating that Jesus was not only before him in time but also holds absolute primacy over him. Had John merely stated that Jesus preceded him, it would solely indicate Jesus' eternity. Yet John asserts that Jesus possesses not only eternity but absolute preeminence, a clear affirmation of His unqualified deity in all respects. This is fitting for Yahweh, the God of the Old Testament.

It is essential to note that the Gospel of John emphasizes Christ's absolute primacy, as part of presenting the Gospel. He is not just portrayed as a gracious Savior but as the supreme sovereign Lord above all. To fully appreciate the salvation He offers, one must first recognize His supreme authority and divine nature.

The Grace

16 For from his fullness we have all received, grace instead of grace.

Christ is a boundless wellspring of covenant steadfast love, grace, truth, and faithfulness. From Him, all who received Him, as referenced in verse 12, received grace instead of grace. It proves indispensable to recognize that this means grace instead of grace,[24] not simply grace upon grace. The law bestowed in the Old Testament constituted a gracious offering from God, yet the offering of Christ transcends it in all respects.

When we reflect upon the grace God extended to the people of the Old Testament, it grows manifest that we stand exceedingly favored. Through the incarnation and completed work of the Lord Jesus upon the cross, we have encountered a preeminent grace.

---

[24] See D. A. Carson, *Gospel According to John*, 131-132, for the articulation of 'grace instead of grace' as the preferable rendering of John 1:16.

17 For the law was given through Moses; grace and truth came through Jesus Christ.

A notable differentiation between the grace of the Old Testament and the preeminent grace of the New Testament rests in the selection of verbs. When describing the Law and Moses, the divine passive verb "was given" is employed. This selection reveals that Christ Himself was the source of grace even in the Old Testament, with Moses acting merely as an instrument of God, a servant of Christ. As Hebrews 3:5-6 clarifies, "Moses was faithful as a servant in God's house, while Christ is faithful as a Son over God's house." This illuminates the preeminence of Christ's grace in the New Testament, affirming His ultimate authority and the surpassing grace brought through His incarnation and redemptive work.

Yet when portraying grace and truth in relation to Christ, the verb "became" finds use, demonstrating that Christ not only originates all grace and truth but also embodies them. The superior grace rests upon the reality that the source and embodiment of grace has incarnated, and from Him directly, we have obtained grace instead of grace. Hence, all goodness within the Law proceeded from Christ. Yet, as Christ embodies grace, the good things of the Old Testament were merely shadows and types of Him and the better things to come. This is echoed in Ephesians 1, which speaks of the redemption we have in Christ according to the riches of His grace, which He lavished upon us.

God the Son

18 No one has ever seen God; the unique, beloved God, who is in the bosom of the Father, He has exegeted Him.

Observe that this verse refers to the unique beloved God and not Jesus Christ. The emphasis here is on God the Son, rather than solely focusing on the incarnation by referring to Jesus Christ. The Son did not become the Word in the incarnation; He has eternally existed as the Word. Yet through the incarnation that we have experienced Him as the Word in utmost fullness. Although the incarnation rendered Him more manifest to us, the Son has perpetually fulfilled a distinctive role within the Triune God as the one revealing God, even prior to the incarnation. Comprehending the Son's revelation of the Triune God with greater fullness in the incarnation necessitates examining the entire prologue in conjunction with verse 18. Though the theophanies of the Old Testament proved partial and transient, God the Son, not God the Father, manifested Himself to the prophets.

This interpretation accords with John 1:1, which declares the Son as the Word who is God. Therefore, John 1:18 is a restatement of John 1:1, affirming that the Son, the unique beloved God, exegetes the Father. Within the full context of the Prologue, the incarnation is where He exegeted the Father most profoundly.

Moreover, a striking parallel exists between John 1:1b, where the Word is with the Father, and John 1:18, where the Son is in the bosom of the Father. John 1:1b depicts the loving eternal relationship between the Son and the Father, and John 1:18 communicates this identical truth. This correspondence affirms that the Son, as the Word, reveals the Father, as evidenced in both verses: "No one has seen the Father but the Son exegeted Him." It affirms the declaration that the Son is God and illuminates the unique relationship between the Son and the Father. All of this demonstrates that John 1:18 restates and emphasizes the components of John 1:1.

A purpose underlies why John 1:1-18 functions as the Prologue: it sets the stage for the entire Gospel. The Gospel of John does not end with these verses but continues through 21 chapters, detailing and fulfilling what is introduced here. Within the fabric of John's Prologue, strands of creation, incarnation, and revelation intertwine, yet the cross and resurrection bestow upon this design its consummate meaning and intent. These events constitute the pinnacle of the divine narrative, where the love, grace, and life-bestowing power of the Word find complete manifestation. The cross is where the attributes of God are supremely displayed—His glory, His grace, His justice, and His love. Believing in the name of Christ means trusting the completed work He accomplished through His life, death on the cross, and resurrection.

Bibliography

Amari, Daniel. Dawn of Islam. *Religion Research Institute, 2020.*

—. John's Logos. *Religion Research Institute, 2019.*

—. Presenting the Gospel to Muslims. *Religion Research Institute, 2024.*

Borchert, Gerald L. John 1-11. *Vol. 25A, in* The New American Commentary, *edited by E. Ray Clendenen, & David S. Dockery. Nashville: Broadman & Holman Publishers, 1996.*

Carson, D. A. The Gospel According to John. *Grand Rapids: Eerdmans, 1991.*

Keener, Craig. The Gospel of John: A Commentary. *Peabody, MA: Hendrickson Publishers, 2003.*

Kruse, Colin G. John: An Introduction and Commentary. *Vol. 4, in* Tyndale New Testament Commenatries. *Downers Grove: InterVarsity Press, 2003.*

Morris, Leon. The Gospel of John. *Grand Rapids: Eerdmans, 1980.*

Porter, Stanley E. The Language of the New Testament: Context, History, and Development. *Leiden: Brill, 2013.*